India

Lisa Zamosky

Publishing Credits

Content Consultant
Radhika Srinivasan

Associate Editor
Christina Hill, M.A.

Assistant Editor
Torrey Maloof

Editorial Assistants
Deborah Buchanan
Kathryn R. Kiley
Judy Tan

Editorial Director
Emily R. Smith, M.A.Ed.

Editor-in-Chief
Sharon Coan, M.S.Ed.

Editorial Manager
Gisela Lee, M.A.

Creative Director
Lee Aucoin

Cover Designer
Lesley Palmer

Designers
Deb Brown
Zac Calbert
Amy Couch
Robin Erickson
Neri Garcia

Publisher
Rachelle Cracchiolo, M.S.Ed.

Teacher Created Materials
5301 Oceanus Drive
Huntington Beach, CA 92649-1030
http://www.tcmpub.com
ISBN 978-0-7439-0430-8
© 2007 Teacher Created Materials, Inc.

Table of Contents

A Long History

India has a special history. Its history is very closely tied to its location. India is between the East and the West. This location has made it a natural place for **invaders** (in-VADE-uhrz). Each group that invaded the country changed it in some way.

India fought in many wars. Different families have ruled over the land. It seems that India is too big and complex for any one group to rule it for long.

People have lived in India for thousands of years. Every group has brought its own **traditions** to the country. These very different traditions have all become part of Indian culture. They have helped to create a very rich society.

Elephants are ▶ important for traditional religious ceremonies.

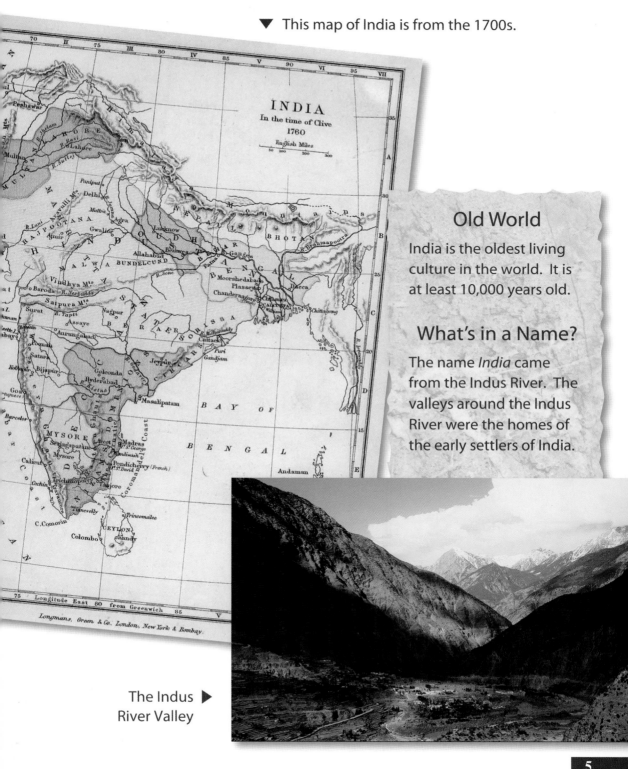

This map of India is from the 1700s.

Old World

India is the oldest living culture in the world. It is at least 10,000 years old.

What's in a Name?

The name *India* came from the Indus River. The valleys around the Indus River were the homes of the early settlers of India.

The Indus ▶ River Valley

Early Invasions

The earliest people in India lived in the south and central parts of the country. They were called Dravidians (druh-VID-ee-uhnz). The **descendents** (dih-SEN-duhntz) of these early settlers still live in southern India today.

A second group of early settlers came to the Indus Valley. Today, this area is in the country of Pakistan (PA-kih-stan). These tribes came from central Europe and Asia. They called themselves the Aryans (AH-ree-uhnz). The word *Aryan* means "noble ones." This group of people lived in the Indus Valley for more than 1,000 years.

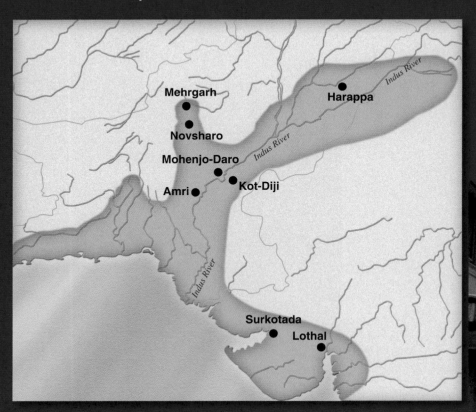

▲ Map of the ancient Indus Valley

◀ This is an example of Dravidian architecture.

The First People

The Aryan and Dravidian societies were the beginning of Indian culture as it exists today.

India Today

India is the world's oldest, largest, continuous **civilization** (siv-uh-luh-ZAY-shuhn).

▲ India today is a crowded country.

The Aryans

The Aryans spread throughout northern India. Many of them wandered through the country raising cattle. Some settled in villages. They invaded the Indus Valley. This pushed the Dravidian people farther south. The Dravidians who stayed started living like the Aryans. Aryans also took on some **customs** of the Dravidian people.

When the Aryans **conquered** (KAN-kuhrd) the people of the Indus Valley, they became the rulers. They set up a **caste system**. The caste system set up different levels for people in society. The Aryans also developed a language. It was called Sanskrit (SAN-skrit). This is one of the oldest languages in the world.

This tablet shows ▶
Sanskrit carvings.

▼ Guards like this one were part of the second level of the caste system.

Speaking the Same Language

Most of the languages spoken in the northern part of India today come from Sanskrit. Even though they come from the same language, the languages sound very different. Sometimes, Indians from different parts of the country will speak English to one another.

Old System in Modern Times

The caste system was officially stopped in India in 1950. But, it still affects who people choose to marry.

▼ Cattle were very important in ancient India.

More Invasions

The Aryan people developed the Hindu religion. Some of the important Hindu gods were Shiva, Kali, and Brahma (BRAH-muh). The Aryans recorded the first **sacred** (SAY-kruhd) Hindu **scriptures** (SKRIP-shuhrz). The scriptures were written in Sanskrit.

The second great invasion of India occurred around 500 B.C. The king of Persia (PURR-zhuh) was Darius (duh-RI-uhs). He conquered the Indus Valley and West Punjab (puhn-JAB). His armies ruled both areas until he died. The Persians continued to rule for 150 years.

Next, the Greeks attacked the Persians. Alexander the Great overthrew King Darius's family. But, the Indians fought Alexander with a strong force. The Greeks left India and returned home.

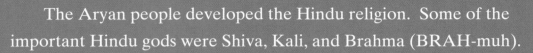

◀ The Hindu gods were honored by the Aryans and other Hindus.

Indians still have shrines like this for Brahma.

Ancient Writing

Indian writing can be traced back nearly 3,000 years to the Hindu scriptures. Today in India, Hindu writers enjoy retelling the tales of the gods in new and exciting ways.

Buddha

Around 563 B.C., a man named Siddhartha Gautama (sihd-DAHR-tuh GAU-tuh-muh) was born in India. He is better known as The Buddha. He preached his beliefs about a balanced life. This is how the religion of **Buddhism** (BOO-dih-zuhm) began.

Buddhism is popular throughout Asia. This is the Great Buddha in Japan.

The Mauryan Empire

Before the Greeks invaded the Indus Valley, a kingdom had developed in northern India. The kingdom grew again once the Greeks left. This was the start of one of India's greatest **dynasties** (DI-nuhs-teez). It was known as the Mauryan (MOR-yuhn) Empire. The first ruler of this empire was Chandragupta (chuhn-druh-GOOP-tuh).

The Mauryas spread across most of northern India. This empire had a huge army. Its government was very organized. The government had a strict system of tax collection. And, the leaders led very comfortable lives. However, life for the **peasants** (PEZ-uhntz) was hard. The Mauryas ruled for about 140 years (321–185 B.C.).

▼ Art from the Mauryan Empire

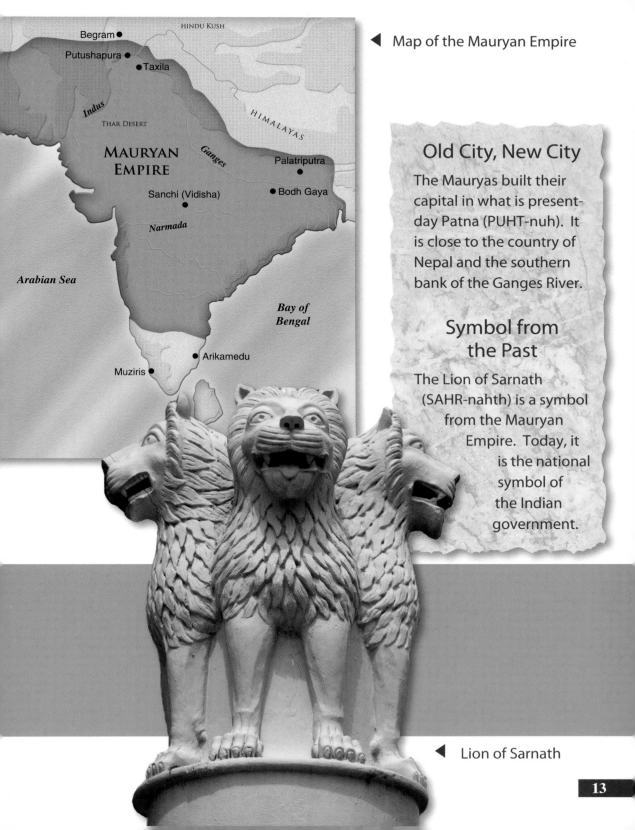

Map of the Mauryan Empire

HINDU KUSH

Begram
Putushapura
Taxila

Indus

THAR DESERT

HIMALAYAS

MAURYAN EMPIRE

Ganges

Palatriputra

Sanchi (Vidisha)

Bodh Gaya

Narmada

Arabian Sea

Bay of Bengal

Arikamedu

Muziris

Old City, New City

The Mauryas built their capital in what is present-day Patna (PUHT-nuh). It is close to the country of Nepal and the southern bank of the Ganges River.

Symbol from the Past

The Lion of Sarnath (SAHR-nahth) is a symbol from the Mauryan Empire. Today, it is the national symbol of the Indian government.

Lion of Sarnath

Ashoka's Rule

The height of the Mauryan Empire was under King Ashoka (ah-SHOW-kuh). He was the grandson of Chandragupta. He was the last great ruler of this dynasty. While he was king, the Mauryan Empire conquered nearly all of India. There were many bloody battles. The king was very upset by what he saw. So, he gave up **warfare** forever. And, he converted to Buddhism.

Ashoka was very committed to teaching people about Buddhism. He brought Buddhism to much of central Asia. He insisted on nonviolence to humans and animals.

His rule of the Mauryan Empire was during its strongest period. The empire collapsed less than 100 years after his death.

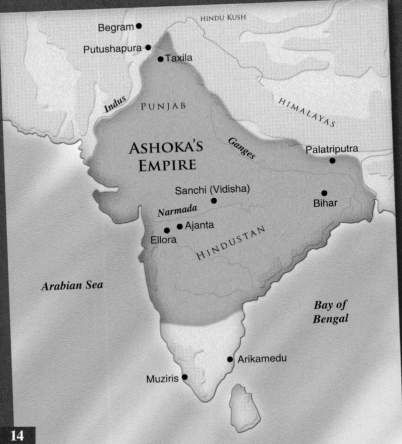

◀ This map shows Ashoka's Empire.

Buddhists Home

Ashoka spread Buddhism among the Indian people. Today, only a small number of Indian people are Buddhists. But, it is an important religion around the world. India is seen as the birthplace of the religion. Buddhists from all over the world travel to India to worship.

Standing Tradition

Sanchi Stupa was a Buddhist shrine built by King Ashoka. It is one of the oldest and most sacred Buddist shrines in the world today.

▲ These women are visiting a Buddhist holy site in India.

▼ Sanchi Stupa

The Gupta Empire

The collapse of the Mauryan dynasty was important. Northern India split into hundreds of separate kingdoms. Foreign invaders ruled most of central and northern India.

Sometimes the kingdoms fought together. They fought invaders from the north and China. But, mostly they stayed separate.

In A.D. 319, King Chandragupta I founded the Gupta (GOOP-tuh) Empire. (This is a different man than Chandragupta from the Mauryan Empire.) He brought together the entire northern part of India. In time, the Guptas spread as far west as the Arabian Sea. And, they went south to the Vindhya (VIN-dyuh) Mountains.

HINDU KUSH

Begram

Putushapura

Taxila

Indus

HIMALAYAS

GUPTA EMPIRE

Ganges

Palatriputra

Sanchi (Vidisha)

Narmada

Bihar

Ajanta

Arabian Sea

Bay of Bengal

Arikamedu

Muziris

The Ajanta Cave ▶ paintings were created during the Gupta Empire.

◀ Map of the Gupta Empire

▲ Art from the Gupta Empire

Zero = Big Change

During the Gupta Empire the math term zero was discovered. This changed mathematics around the world forever.

Great Indian Art

The Ajanta (uh-JUHN-tuh) Cave has paintings made during this period. They represent the various lives of Buddha. They are also the best source of what daily life in India was like during that time. To this day, they are considered among the greatest works of Indian art.

Chandragupta II

The Gupta Empire reached its peak under the leadership of Chandragupta II. Chandragupta II was responsible for building universities. He also built some of India's most incredible temples.

Chandragupta II encouraged his people to study art and science. He wanted them to paint, sculpt, and read. Many scientific gains were made in India during this time. This was a peaceful, stable time in India. It is known as the "golden age."

Chandragupta II ruled for about 45 years. The Gupta Empire lasted until around the year A.D. 550. Then, the White Huns from central Asia defeated the Guptas. After the Gupta Empire fell, India broke apart again. Over time, it became many separate Hindu kingdoms.

▼ These are the ruins of a temple built by Chandragupta II.

Chandragupta Gold

Chandragupta II made many gold coins during his time as ruler. In fact, the largest number of Gupta coins found in India today were made during his **reign** (RAIN).

Hindu Temples

Many important Hindu temples throughout India today were built just after the Gupta Empire.

▼ Hindu temple today

The Mughal Empire

The next 1,000 years were a time of great conflict in India. **Muslims** (MUHZ-luhmz) invaded India several times. In 1526, India came under Muslim control from central Asia. Then, **Mongols** (MAHN-guhlz) invaded northern India. They began an empire called the Mughal (MUH-guhl) Empire. Their first leader was Babur (BAH-buhr).

▼ Babur was a strong leader.

▲ The Taj Mahal was built in the 1600s.

Babur was only one of many successful leaders in the Mughal Empire. Akbar (AK-buhr) was considered the greatest of all Mughal rulers. The empire spread through northern India and parts of the south. All of this happened over a period of about 200 years.

The Mughals did not destroy the ways of life in the places where they took control. They allowed the Indians to keep their traditions. The Mughals loved to build. They built many important structures in the country. The empire ended by the 1800s.

Taj Mahal

The Taj Mahal (TAJ MAH-hall) may be the most famous of all buildings in India. It is actually one of the most famous in the world. It was built by Emperor Shah Jahan (SHAH juh-HAHN) as a tomb for his favorite wife. It still stands today in Agra, India. Tourists come from all around the world every year to visit the Taj Mahal.

The Red Fort

The Red Fort in New Delhi was built during the Mughal Empire. It is perhaps the most recognized building in New Delhi today.

Great Britain Takes Control

By the early 1800s, Great Britain had moved into India. Britain had set up a company called the East India Company. Leaders who were chosen by the British government ruled the company.

The East India Company controlled about half of India. Indian princes controlled the other half of the country. These princes promised to be loyal to Great Britain.

The British caused many changes in India. Some changes were good for Indians. The British built hospitals and schools throughout the country. They also paved roads and built railway systems. The Indian Civil Service was created by the British. This gave Indians good-paying jobs.

Other changes hurt the people in India. And, the Indians were not happy with the British.

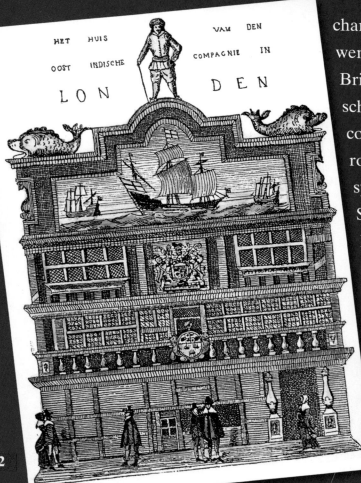

HET HUIS VAN DEN
OOST INDISCHE COMPAGNIE IN
LON DEN

◀ The East India Company headquarters in London

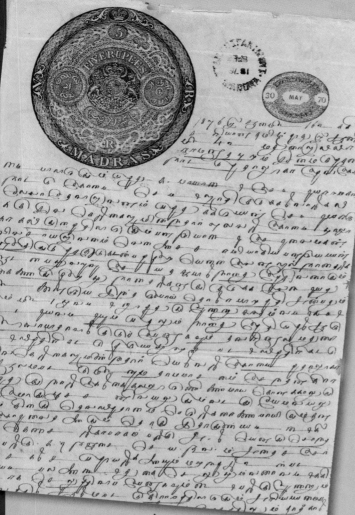

This is an East ▲
India Company
document.

Good Jobs

The Indian Administration Service replaced the Indian Civil Service in the late 1940s. The Administration Service is still a source of jobs for Indians.

British Built

Many of the structures built by the British were not available to the Indian people during British rule. However, some of the hospitals and roads built by the British are being used by Indian people today.

The Indian ▶
Parliament in
New Delhi was
built by British
architects.

Indians Rise Up

The Indian people were not always treated fairly by the British. Laws were passed that kept Indians from high posts in government. Many people lost their land because they were unable to pay the high taxes.

Indians ▶ fight the British

Some British people were not sensitive to Indian religious practices. The British citizens often lived in wealthy towns, while the Indians were living in **slums**. Indians were unhappy under British rule.

In 1857, a rumor spread among Indian soldiers serving in the British army. The rumor said that their bullets had been greased with animal fat. Some people heard it was pig fat. Others heard it was the fat of cows. People in the Islam religion find pigs unclean. And, cows are considered holy to Hindus. So, both Muslims and Hindus thought that this was an insult. Indian soldiers began to fight the British. When the fighting was over, the East India Company ended.

Holy Cow

Eating cows is against the law in several states in India today because it is against Hindu beliefs.

A Different Kind of Burger

In 1996, McDonald's opened its first beefless restaurant in New Delhi. It offered a "mutton burger," which is made from sheep. This was meant to appeal to Muslims who will not eat pork and to Hindus who will not eat beef.

Independence

Control of India still belonged to the British government. But, the Indians wanted to rule themselves. In 1885, the India National Congress was formed. It was a political party that fought against British rule. The All-India Muslim League was also formed. This group fought for the rights of Muslims. They wanted their own nation. The British talked about giving Indians control. At the same time, they passed laws that took away Indians' rights.

Mohandas Gandhi (mo-HAWN-duhs GAWN-dee) was a lawyer from a wealthy Hindu family. He dedicated his life to fighting for India's independence from Britain. He used nonviolent ways of fighting. He gave speeches and held marches.

On August 15, 1947, India gained independence. Gandhi lived to see this. Sadly, a fellow Hindu shot him. He died in 1948.

In 1950, a new **constitution** was developed. India had a free, independent government.

◀ Celebrating India's Independence Day

Gandhi and others march to protest against the government.

Father Gandhi

Gandhi was also known by the name Mahatma (muh-HAHT-muh). This means "father of a nation."

▼ People in India today have a lot of freedoms.

A Free India

Since winning their independence in 1950, Indians enjoy voting rights and freedom of speech, religion, and the press.

A Model Government

Today, the Indian legislature is modeled after Great Britain's **parliamentary** (pawr-luh-MEN-tuh-ree) **system**.

Moving Into the Modern World

Jawaharlal Nehru (juw-AH-url-ahl NAY-roo) became India's first prime minister. There have been many leaders since that time. One of these rulers was Nehru's daughter, Indira Gandhi. She became prime minister in 1966. She led the country for many years. However, because she abused her power, she was voted out of office.

India is a complex country. Poverty and a very large population remain big problems in the country. So does hatred among different religious groups. There are many problems among the Hindus, Muslims, and

Jawaharlal Nehru

Indira Gandhi

Sikhs (SEEKZ). The Sikhs are another popular religious group in India.

India has grown a lot since gaining its independence. It has a very rich history and many cultures. India holds an important place in the modern world.

Once the Richest

India was one of the richest countries of the world until the time of the British.

Number 6

India is the sixth largest country in the world. It has the second largest population, just behind China.

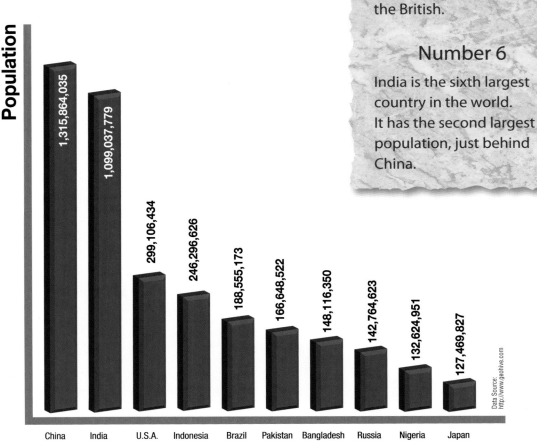

Population

- China 1,315,864,035
- India 1,099,037,779
- U.S.A. 299,106,434
- Indonesia 246,296,626
- Brazil 188,555,173
- Pakistan 166,648,522
- Bangladesh 148,116,350
- Russia 142,764,623
- Nigeria 132,624,951
- Japan 127,469,827

Data Source:
http://www.geohive.com

Population of the 10 Largest Countries in the World

Glossary

Buddhism—a religion that began in India and follows the teachings of Buddha

caste system—a social system in which class is decided by a person's family

civilization—a society that has writing and keeps track of records

conquered—overcame by force

constitution—the system of laws that rule a government

customs—practices followed by people of a particular group or region

descendents—people who come from a particular family

dynasties—families that hold power for many years

invaders—people who enter by force as an enemy

Mongols—people from Mongolia

Muslims—people who believe in the religion of Islam

parliamentary system—the rules followed by the government when holding its meetings

peasants—poor people who live in the countryside

reign—the time period that a king or queen rules

sacred—items or beliefs considered very important to a religion

scriptures—writings that are very important to the religious beliefs of a group of people

Sikhs—people who follow a religion based in northern India

slums—housing areas where poor people live in bad conditions

traditions—parts of culture that are passed from older people to younger people

warfare—military struggles between nations or groups

Index

Image Credits